CW00853092

THE 13TH ZODIAC
(OPHIUCHUS)

AND

THE GALACTIC SOLAR SYSTEM

UNVEILED

BY

KWAME OSEI-GHANSAH
(AMORIFER)

Bloomington, IN  Milton Keynes, UK

authorHOUSE®

AuthorHouse™
1663 Liberty Drive, Suite 200
Bloomington, IN 47403
www.authorhouse.com
Phone: 1-800-839-8640

AuthorHouse™ *UK Ltd.*
500 Avebury Boulevard
Central Milton Keynes, MK9 2BE
www.authorhouse.co.uk
Phone: 08001974150

First published by AuthorHouse 9/13/2006

ISBN: 1-4259-5809-5 (e)
ISBN: 1-4259-5808-7 (sc)

Printed in the United States of America
Bloomington, Indiana

This book is printed on acid-free paper.

TABLE OF CONTENTS

BY WAY OF INTRODUCTION

By the time one finishes reading the book the following astronomically and cosmographically verifiable facts emerge:

1. There are 28 days to each lunar month.

2. There are 364 days to each lunar year.

3. There are 13 months to each lunar year.

4. It is the STARRY DESIGNS that form the background to each lunar month that constitute the ZODIAC SIGNS.

5. There are therefore THIRTEEN ZODIAC SIGNS.

6. OPHIUCHIUS – The Serpent Holder – which is between Scorpio and Sagittarius, is the one which has been denied existence.

7. 'Thirty Days Hath September, April, June, and November ……..' is a FALSE TEACHING.

8. The LEAP DAY, and LEAP YEAR are not valid (No moon – cycle is 29 days long).

9. SEPTEMBER is rather the SEVENTH MONTH (sept-septem).

10. OCTOBER is rather the EIGHTH MONTH.

11. DECEMBER is rather the TENTH MONTH (Decimal – Decade – Decem).

12. FEBRUARY is rather the THIRTEENTH MONTH.

13. ALL OUR BIRTHDATES ARE FALSE.

14. ALL OUR ZODIAC SIGNS ARE FALSE.

15. OUR CALENDAR NEEDS TO BE OVERHAULED.

16. The KNIGHTS TEMPLAR MASSACRE on Friday the 13th of October, 1307, which made Friday the 13th and the number 13 unlucky for Euroamericans, is what is behind these FALSIFICATIONS.

NOW TO THE COSMOGRAPHICAL DISCOVERIES

17. The ZODIAC SIGNS INSIDE OUR planetary GALAXY are duplicated inside our GALACTIC GALAXY.

18. The PLANETARY SOLAR SYSTEM is duplicated by the GALACTIC SOLAR SYSTEM.

19. There is such a thing as a GALACTIC SUN which is different from a planetary GALAXY even though they all appear as ISLANDS OF LIGHT in infinite space.

20. The smallest possible UNIT recognizable throughout SPACE, when one peeps through The Hale Telescope is a BALL OF LIGHT/AN ISLAND OF LIGHT.

21. We are not part of the Milky Way Galaxy, since we have a SIDE-VIEW picture snapped through the Hale Telescope.

22. There is no such thing as a SEPARATE SOLAR SYSTEM or a SEPARABLE SOLAR SYSTEM.

23. Actually A Planetary GALAXY is a group of PLANETARY SOLAR SYSTEMS.

24. Which makes a GALACTIC GALAXY a group of GALACTIC SOLAR SYSTEMS.

25. The 2000 year NEW AGES can be seen clearly only after the GALACTIC SOLAR SYSTEM makes it possible for our Planetary GALAXY to orbit its GALACTIC SUN over a period of 26,000 years.

26. That makes each of the 13 Greater ZODIAC SIGNS last exactly 2,000 years as the planetary Galaxy journeys around its sun. (Our so-called Millenium).

27. The PRECESSION OF THE EQUINOXES is a joke that can only happen inside the roof of our own planetary GALAXY.

28. **THE BIG BANG is a falsehood because it needs a "PREVIOUSLY CREATED" STAR system to contract to the point where THE EXPLOSION needed for creation to "START" becomes possible.**

29. The GOD – CYCLE which is as hermetically – sealed as THE GALAXIES – CYCLE and the WATER – CYCLE, takes care of the BIG – BANG FALSE SCIENCE.

30. THE GOD ORGANISM HAS NO DISCERNIBLE BEGINNING NOR ENDING.

31. **HUBBLE'S EFFECT does not indicate an expanding or a contracting universe. It only indicates when a whole planetary GALAXY in our Galactic Solar System is either moving away or**

coming closer to our own planetary Galaxy.

32. Just as our planet is trapped in our Solar System and inside our planetary Galaxy; our planetary Galaxy is trapped inside our Galactic Solar System and our Galactic Galaxy.

33. In fact, just as NO DROP OF WATER (W) ever escapes outside our WATER – CYCLE, NO DROP OF MATTER (M) escapes outside the Galaxies – Cycle and NO DROP OF SOUL (S) escapes outside the GOD – CYCLE.

*   *   *

All you need to accept this **SCIENTIFIC BREAKTHROUGH** is to consult Astronomers who have access to the Hale Telescope on Mount Palomar, California(U.S.A), (or even Astronomy Lecturers).

Galileo discovered that the planet was in double motion in 1633. I have discovered that the Planetary Galaxy is ALSO IN DOUBLE MOTION inside both our Galactic Solar System and our Galactic Galaxy.

PRELUDE TO BOOK ONE

OPHIUCHUS UNVEILED

Do you have an exercise book nearby? Go to the back cover, to that portion titled "TIME MEASURE": At the very bottom, you will see "12 calendar months or 13 lunar months make one year" . The truth is that the Ancient Egyptians drew the 13 designs- patterns behind each of the 13 lunar months and ended up with the 13 SIGNS OF THE ZODIAC : -

1.	ARIES	--	The Ram
2.	TAURUS	--	The Bull
3.	GEMINI	--	The Twins
4.	CANCER	--	The Crab
5.	LEO	--	The Lion
6.	VIRGO	--	The Virgin
7.	LIBRA	--	The Balance
8.	SCORPIO	--	The Scorpion
9.	OPHIUCHUS	--	The Serpent Holder
10.	SAGITTARIUS	--	The Archer
11.	CAPRICORNUS	--	The Goat
12.	AQUARIUS	--	The Water Carrier
13.	PISCES	--	The Fishes

And there were exactly 13 months, too. Each month was exactly 28 days long. There was no such thing as the 29th, 30th, or 31st, days of the month. There was nothing like a LEAP DAY or A LEAP YEAR, because there is still no moon – cycle that is 29 days long. That was when SEPT- SEPTEM – SEPTEMBER was the SEVENTH month and OCTO- OCTOPUS – OCTOBER was the EIGHTH month.

From today onwards, study each moon – cycle and the starry patterns that form the background to each of the 28 – day , thirteen LUNAR MONTHS of the year. With the 13 lunar months come the 13 SIGNS OF THE ZODIAC.

Between Scorpio and Sagittarius lies OPHIUCHUS – The Serpent Holder-which has been denied EXISTENCE since Friday, the 13th of October, 1307, even though it is still up there ,in VOIDGOD'S NIGHT SKY.

Yes , even as you read these lines.

It is still part of the STARS that constitute our PLANETARY GALAXY OF STARS AND THEIR ENCIRCLING PLANETS.

OPHIUCHUS wants to be recognized, reinstated................

OPHIUCHUS wants to tell its side of the story.

- AMORIFER -

BOOK ONE

THE 13 LUNAR MONTHS AND THE 13 ZODIAC SIGNS

"True knowledge consists in a direct recognition of the   TRUTH   and is taught by Nature herself"

- Unknown Author –

"When I sit down to write, I do not say to myself I am going to produce a work of art. I write because there is some UNTRUTH that I want to EXPOSE, some (OPHIUCHUS) (GALACTIC SOLAR SYSTEM) fact to which I want to draw attention and my initial concern is to get a HEARING."

- George Orwell -
(Credit : Yaw Boadu Ayeboafoh)

*   *   *

Ever since I became conscious of my surroundings as a child, it is the stars of the night that have fascinated me the most. It took me so many years to realize that they have maintained their positions ever since I started seeing them.

THEN CAME THE MOON and its ever-changing shapes that also never changed. Every first day of the moon has its shape that is always the same. Every seventh day of the moon predictably produces the HALF - MOON. And every fourteenth day of the moon always produces the first FULL MOON.

l started playing a game with the moon when I was about eight years old. I used to pick stones to count the number of days it took for the moon to appear anew . I always ended up with twenty eight stones. The twenty ninth stone always ended up being my next FIRST STONE.

THEN CAME THE RAINY SEASON. The rains were also reporting for duty after exactly thirteen moon – cycles. I had extended my stone picking game with the moon – cycle to that of the rainy season by the time I was twelve years old . I was not aware of the other natural changes like the HARMATTAN and the rest, because they never announced themselves in dramatic fashion. The other seasons did not make any serious impression upon my child mind because they had nothing to do with the planting of corn or the planting of yams.

By the time I was twelve years old , my thirteen BIG STONES for the moon – cycles before the next rainy season, had made me know that there were exactly thirteen lunar months of twenty eight days each, to each lunar year.

My Geography Teachers could never convince me of the LEAP DAY or the LEAP YEAR. (Which of the moon – cycles was giving them the 29th day ?) I was always laughing whenever I heard the innocent and ignorant Primary School children chanting:

"THIRTY DAYS HATH SEPTEMBER , APRIL, JUNE AND NOVEMBER, ALL THE REST HAVE THIRTY – ONE……."

I used to look up at the sky , at the VOIDGOD (ONYAME A OHATA HO YI) and assured IT that I was going to rectify that falsification of natural truth, one fine day. There is no moon – cycle (month) that is even twenty – nine days long. So what are all these thirty and thirty one days in aid of ? To my natural mind there was no moon – cycle up there in VOIDGOD'S SKY , which could answer to that 29th day.

Matters got worse for my Geography Teachers when they started forcing me to accept 365 and 366 days to one year. I knew of only 364 days flat. But I always wrote their wrong and false answers for them to get my hundred per cent, with a smile in my heart. I would laugh at the ignorant Teachers under my breath and assure the VOIDGOD that when I grew up and had the opportunity, I would restore the thirteen months of the year and the three hundred and sixty four days, TRUTHS.

I did not then know of the thirteen signs of the zodiac. You see, my fascination with the stars did not imprint on my child mind the possibility of specific and particular artistic designs up there. I saw the Canis Major and the Canis Minor, alright. But beyond those two " FLAGS"; the stars were scattered all over the place and did not form any particular patterns.

It was my interest in ' THE STARS AND YOU ' that appeared in the various newspapers that got me looking out for Astrology and Astronomy books. That was when it struck me that the ZODIAC SIGNS were the different starry patterns or designs that formed behind every new moon- cycle.

YOU SEE , IT IS ALMOST IMPOSSIBLE TO ACCEPT THAT OUR PLANET IS ORBITTING OUR SUN / STAR, WITHOUT SEEING THE NEW STARRY PATTERNS UP THERE, IN THE NIGHT- TIME SKY (OF THE VOIDGOD), WHICH ACCOMPANY EVERY NEW MOON- CYCLE.

To my child mind, the new moon and the resultant full moon, were always appearing IN THE SAME PLACE in the sky. UNTIL THE Astrology and Astronomy books started telling me that those of us born from the 23rd of September to the 19th of October, were LIBRANS, I could not factor the movement of the planet ROUND THE SUN, into my world –view. In fact , only the sun moved from East to West every day of my life as a child and even as a young man(It looks as if Mother Nature is always laughing at us. The unmoving SUN is made to seem TO MOVE. And the MOVING PLANET is so STATIONARY. No wonder I never associated MOTION with the GALAXY OF STARS. It looks so STATIONARY!)

The problems I had with my Geography Teachers cropped up again. Here I was, two hundred per cent sure that every STAR SIGN or ZODIAC SIGN coincided with one moon- cycle. Here was I, three hundred per cent sure that each zodiac sign started and ended with one moon-cycle. Here was l , four hundred per cent sure that the dates should have been the FIRST of this or that month, to the TWENTY EIGHTH of this or that month.

Here was I being told by LINDA GOODMAN and company that there were ONLY twelve zodiac signs and most annoyingly, that they started from the middle of their new false twelve months and not from the first day of the new moon-cycle.

You remember how I promised the VOIDGOD (ONYAME A ɔHATA Hɔ YI) that l would rectify the twelve months of the year when l was about twelve years old? Well, this time l was in my twenties and being preoccupied with more USELESS INFORMATION and DATA that l had to learn BY ROTE and reproduce to get a university degree.

I had so much trouble with my capitalist oriented Economics Lecturers that l still BLESS THE DAY the Department of French of the University of Cape Coast –Ghana –came to bail me out with the option of an honours course in French.

One Economics Lecturer told me to my face that if l had written one particular paper in Moscow or Havana, they would have given me a straight " A', but since the paper was being graded in Ghana, the "D" he was giving me was even for my English and my handwriting. Of course, l am writing this piece in English because l despise THE GOVERNMENT OF FRANCE and their ASSIMILATIONIST policy. Can you imagine anyone being capable of UNMAKING the natural Black African Mentality that is me? I cannot be brainwashed. I am an expert at AUTO –HYPNOSIS.

These days l can understand all the french that l hear, but to get me to speak french correctly for five minutes is a job even the VOIDGOD cannot do. I hold in perfect CONTEMPT the French and their destruction of all foreign, native, industries as epitomized in Eric Van Lustbader's FRENCH KISS.

I simply cannot tolerate injustice and intentional immorality. Selfishness that is SELF- PRESERVATIONIST IS OKAY. But Selfishness that thrives on the destruction of ALL OTHER PEOPLES' VALUES AND LIVES, is reprehensible. And as far as I am concerned, THE DEVIL I KNOW SHOULD NEVER BE ALLOWED TO COME NEAR ME.

So I came face to face with modern Astrologers who were trying to compel me to accept twelve zodiac signs when I knew, for sure, that there were thirteen of them in the NIGHT – TIME SKY OF THE VOIDGOD.

I started journeying with the planet around the sun inside THE PLANETARY GALAXY. I started greeting the new signs of the ZODIAC inside THE PLANETARY GALAXY, as I met them with every new moon – cycle. It took me another fifteen years of reading and researching for Henry Lincoln's <u>HOLY BLOOD AND HOLY GRAIL</u> to give me the name and position of the thirteenth zodiac sign. It is on page 100 of that book. It is called OPHIUCHUS – The Serpent Holder. And it is right there, right now, between Scorpio and Sagittarius. Joy is too small a word for what I experienced that day. ECSTASY is also too small.

MENTAL ORGASM will come close, provided we limit it to the very, very, FIRST ORGASMIC PLEASURE. You know how familiarity breeds CONTEMPT for everything and how we can never go back to IXTLAN, dear Carlos Castaneda. You know how the honey moon manufactured child is always more sexually 'rotten' than that child you both had fifteen years after the wedding 'madness'. But how many parents do not stand back in ignorant and HYPOCRITICAL shock, when their own sexual 'madness' child behaves according to the GENETIC IMPULSES they themselves gave the poor boy or girl?!

It took me another ten years before I could see the MAP OF THE STARS in Dr. Baldwin Baddoo's office with the word OPHIUCHUS comfortably perched between those of Scorpio and Sagittarius.

"Nature is the Universal Mother (Teacher) of all, and if you are in harmony with her, if the mirror of your mind has not been made BLIND by the cobwebs of speculations, erroneous (theological / religious) theories, and (racial / racist) misconceptions, she will hold up before you a mirror in which you will see THE TRUTH"
- Unknown Author -

I had journeyed with the planet from one rainy season to another and met all the thirteen signs of the Zodiac. I had come face to face with the reality that with the introduction of the 29th , 30th and 31st dates, something very wrong had happened to ALL BIRTHDATES.

I had equally come face to face with the FALSEHOOD that was the twelve signs of the zodiac, the more so since they were all starting from the middle of the signs instead of the beginning.

NOT ONLY THAT.

WHERE ARE ALL THE OPHIUCHUSIANS?

WHERE HAVE ALL THE OPHIUCHUSIANS GONE ?

Now that some of them are called LIBRANS or SCORPIOS or PISCEANS or SAGITTARIANS, is there a single human being on this planet who truly knows his sign of the zodiac? Is there a single individual on this planet who truly knows his BIRTHDATE especially since we have been practising SHIFTING CULTIVATION for over 700 years?

Let me explain.

1307 ended ONE DAY before it was granted official blessings.
1308 ended TWO DAYS before it was proclaimed.
1309 ended THREE or even FOUR DAYS earlier than it was proclaimed.
WHY?
The new years are 365 and 366 days long instead of 364, you NIT WIT.
Who is behind this joke?
And why 1307?

It took me another ten years to come face to face with the date called Friday, the 13th of October, 1307. They say Friday, the 13th ,is considered as UNLUCKY by Euroamericans. They say it is what happened to THE KNIGHTS TEMPLAR on that Friday, the 13th of October, 1307, that made the Euroamericans consider the number 13, unlucky.

Who was the Roman Catholic Pope who plotted with Francois le Bel of France, to massacre those TENS OF THOUSANDS of the Red Cross Bearing Knights Templar CRUSADERS that midnight to one o'clock of Friday, the 13th of October, 1307?

So, those who did the FALSIFICATION are the Red Cross Bearing CRUSADERS in Euroamerican history. And they did the alteration and falsification of everything 13, after that Friday, the 13th of October, 1307.

THE CALENDAR ...... THE ZODIAC .....
THE GLANDS .... THE THIRTEEN
DISCIPLES OF JESUS .... all tumbled from thirteen to twelve. (There were two Judases. One Iscariot and the other of John 14: 22 (Not Iscariot))

In other words, we can put ourselves before any computer and arrange TWO VERTICAL columns in which we will have two sets of dates. We can have our first set of thirteen months of the year, for the year 1307, ON ONE VERY CRITICAL CONDITION.

The pre – condition of ETERNAL VIGILANCE. WHY?

There is something VERY, VERY, WRONG with the arrangement of their months, as WELL.

I told you I learnt French at the University. Well, I learnt LATIN too, up to my Sixth Form. So I know SEPT – SEPTEM stand for SEVEN in French and Latin, respectively. OCTO stands for EIGHT and the OCTOPUS is so named because it has EIGHT TENTACLES. Then comes NOVEM for NINE in Latin. THEN COMES DECEM which is the Latin for TEN. We still consider the DECADE to be TEN years long.

So why is SEPTEMBER the ninth month instead of the SEVENTH?

So why is OCTOBER the tenth instead of the EIGHTH month ?

So why is NOVEMBER the eleventh instead of the NINTH month ?

So why is DECEMBER the twelfth instead of the TENTH month?

And why is FEBRUARY no longer THE LAST of the THIRTEEN months but has been hopped, stepped and jumped to the SECOND POSITION in their BOGUS CALENDAR?

This means that the new AQUARIAN AGE CALENDAR we have in view, will have October as the EIGHTH MONTH and it will be allotted ONLY 28 DAYS. Then November, December, Ophiuchus, January, and February will also be given 28 DAYS EACH.

Since there is no LEAP DAY to any moon – cycle (NOT UP THERE IN VOIDGOD'S SKY), our true year will be exactly 364 days long. The **ONE FALSE DAY** added TO THE normal year and the **TWO FALSE DAYS** added to the LEAP YEAR, will have to be kept in view so that by the time we reach YEAR 2005 from 1307, everyone will know his TRUE BIRTHDATE and also his TRUE ZODIAC SIGN.

1307 to 2007 is already some 700 years of false astrology, false zodiac signs, FALSE RACE GODS, FALSE RACE SONS OF GOD, and life without OPHIUCHUSIANS.

If we keep the leap day in view, we will be dealing with some EIGHT HUNDRED AND

SEVENTY FIVE (875) STOLEN DAYS. Divided by 364 days, we have been cheated of some TWENTY FIVE (25) YEARS.

Therefore, the calendar should have been reading, 2030!

A

THE VOIDGOD (THE INSTINCTVOIDGOD) IS THE ONLY TRUE SPIRITUALGOD OCEAN IN WHICH GALAXIES LIVE, MOVE AND HAVE THEIR BEINGS------ WITH HUMAN BEINGS CRAWLING ON THEIR BACKS.

B

THE GALACTIC SOLAR SYSTEM HAS ALSO BEEN DISCOVERED. THE KEY TO THE 2000 YEAR AGES SPOKEN ABOUT IN ALL THE ANCIENT BLACK EGYPTIAN LITERATURE.

C

THE GALAXIES- CYCLE (WHICH IS ONE HALF OF THE GOD –CYCLE) WHICH IS AS HERMETICALLY –SEALED AS THE WATER-CYCLE, ELIMINATES THE BIG BANG.

But we are going to FESTINA LENTE

POSTLUDE TO BOOK ONE

CEASING TO BE LABOURED FOR

"Notwithstanding the apparent fact that humanity CHANGES BUT LITTLE, there are great moments when the world really does grow BETTER than it ever was before.

One off these moments is when one of the children ceases to be laboured for and becomes in turn one of the (MENTAL) labourers in the (FRUIT- VEGETABLE- GARDEN) of humanity.

There are one or two in each great civilization who rise to the fuller requirements of LIFE and learn so well the lessons which confront them that they are capable of becoming an INTELLECTUAL POWER for the unfoldment of men, for the upliftment of men.

One who had suffered much, who had toiled long, had felt the anguish of the theologically/ religiously DECEIVED WORLD------had seen the uselessness of material glory; who had performed the GREAT WORK and climbed the lofty (galacto – galacto – galacto – galacto(to the fifth power) galactic galaxy) heights, seeking earnestly to draw others UP TO THE REALMS OF TRUTH. (Pp 84-85)

The Ways of The Lonely Ones by Manly Palmer Hall

PRELUDE TO BOOK TWO

THE HERMETIC PRINCIPLE OF CORRESPONDENCE

''This Hermetic Principle of Correspondence(As Above So Below; As Below So Above) when grasped MENTALLY, gives one the means of solving many a dark paradox, and hidden secret of Nature.

There are planes beyond our knowing, but when we apply the Principle of Correspondence to them we are able to understand much that would otherwise be unknowable to us.

The ancient Hermetists considered this Principle as one of the most IMPORTANT MENTAL INSTRUMENTS by which man was able to PRY ASIDE THE OBSTACLES WHICH HID FROM VIEW the UNKNOWN.

Just as a knowledge of the PRINCIPLE OF GEOMETRY enables man to measure distant SUNS ...... distant GALAXIES ...... and their movements, while seated in his observatory, so a knowledge of the Principle of Correspondence enables man to reason INTELLIGENTLY from the known to the UNKNOWN.

STUDYING THE MONAD, he understands the ARCHANGEL" (PP 28 – 30)

THE KYBALION By Three Initiates)

Let us see if The Three Initiates are correct in their assertions. Studying the GALAXY, can we understand the Galacto – Galacto – Galacto – Galacto - Galacto – Galactic Galaxy?

- AMORIFER -

STILL PRELUDE TO BOOK TWO

THE GALACTIC SOLAR SYSTEM UNVEILED

If you have read some Astrology and Astronomy books, you have been left wondering as to why THE MILLENIUM IS NOT ONE THOUSAND YEARS LONG, BUT TWO.

Deeper students of MYSTICISM must also have been left wondering as to what was meant by the GREATER ZODIAC being 26,000 years long.

Many are the Astrologers and Astronomers who have tried to use a PLEIDEAN SYSTEM and a PRECESSION OF THE EQUINOXES SYSTEM to force these two ideas inside our own galaxy of STARS and their encircling planets.

The Galactic Solar System, where OUR GALAXY is given a SOLAR SYSTEM that duplicates that of our planet, is the first cosmographically POSSIBLE CONSTRUCT, that leaves no one in doubt. It is so ncat and simple IT IS GOING TO MAKE PEOPLE WONDER

WHY THEY NEVER SAW IT WITH THEIR MIND'S EYE.

Cosmographers have seen millions of BALLS OF LIGHT along the ONE SEXTILLION MILE RANGE of the Hale Telescope. All past Cosmographers saw all these BALLS OF LIGHT as GALAXIES OF STARS AND THEIR ORBITTING PLANETS.

I am begging to differ by saying that 100 million of those BALLS OF LIGHT ARE GALACTIC SUNS duplicating our 100 million PLANETARY SUNS inside our GALAXY.

If our past Cosmographers had called our GALAXY, A PLANETARY GALAXY, in that every SUN / STAR is orbited by, at least, SEVEN PLANETS INSIDE OUR GALAXY, they would have been able to see why our 100 million GALACTIC SUNS are orbited by, at least, 700 million PLANETARY GALAXIES, in our GALACTIC GALAXY ………

But I am jumping the gun ……………
                    - AMORIFER -

BOOK TWO

THE GALACTIC SOLAR SYSTEM

When we met at the time the moon was passing through the constellation OPHIUCHUS, I was a relatively young man of some twenty three years old. I was a year or two short of leaving the university and a year or two short of when to start shaking off the tag of INTELLECTUAL PIMP. (That condition in which outsiders, other than ourselves, decide what we should LEARN, what we should BELIEVE, and how to LIVE OUR LIVES).

Carlos Castaneda thought he was superior to Don Juan Matus until his being the STOOGE and PUPPET of professors who had drawn up his syllabuses and, therefore, his whole ACADEMIC DESTINY, dawned on him. That was when he saw that it is more dignifying to live like a HUNTER – WARRIOR where you decide to study the galaxies and galactic solar systems instead of "THE USE OF ENGLISH IN THE GHANAIAN POLITICAL DISCOURSE" (Insincere apologies to Miss Kate Agyei Koranteng of Abetifi – Kwahu)

When you became aware of OPHIUCHUS and his 12 Brethren (Joseph and his 12 Brethren?), you became aware of the PLANETARY GALAXY of 100 million stars / suns and their, at least, 700 million planets that orbit them.

I am now in my mid fifties and still a WALKING QUESTION MARK. I take consolation from the fact that I understand many, many, things that used to baffle me in my youth. "Thirty days hath September, April, June and November …" were true statements before we UNVEILED OPHIUCHUS.

All the STARS you can see at night, from every VANTAGE POINT of the planet (Australia, Patagonia, Antarctic and Arctic Circles inclusive), are part of the PLANETARY GALAXY in which we are traveling through SPACE and TIME.

Never mind that the CONCEPT OF GALAXY hit Euroamerican minds only after 1920 – after Champolion had found the USE for THE ROSETTA STONE that Napoleon's Captain brought from the Port City of ROSETTA, near Alexandria – Egypt!

Also, never mind that in spite of the fact that light travels at 300,000 kilometers per second, it takes light 80,000 years to cover THE DIAMETER of our planetary galaxy. Of course, light covers 18 million kilometers in ONE MINUTE so I have not got the heart to give you, in kilometers, what ONE LIGHT YEAR IS, let alone 80,000 light years .

There are, at least, seven planets orbiting every SUN/ STAR IN OUR planetary galaxy. With 700 million planets inside our planetary galaxy, it takes a lot of common sense IGNORANCE to assume that there are no other human beings on other planets in the other solar systems and even in other galaxies throughout INFINITY. To that extent where even when we see identifiable extra – terrestrial FLYING OBJECTS, we play the OSTRICH by calling the identifiable objects " UNIDENTIFIED FLYING OBJECTS " (UFOS) .

Now that the one sextillion mile range Hale Telescope has shown us PICTURES   of millions of planetary galaxies like the M- 31, the Andromeda, the Magellan and the Milky Way, I am feeling mighty sorry   for the successor to John Paul II. He is bound to be the last Pope since the New Age of Aquarius that this small pamphlet is going to herald into acceptance, will be the Age of SPIRITUAL LAW PRACTITIONERS

(Let me, here, assure all readers that the next time we meet will be when I will explain the workings of the other SIX HERMETIC PRINCIPLES of

1) MENTALISM (Mental Transmutation)
2) VIBRATION
3) POLARITY
4) RHYTHM
5) CAUSE AND EFFECT (Law of Karma)
6) GENDER (Mental Generation)

Those who have had the privilege of peeping through our two telescopes on top of Mounts Palomar (California – USA) and Wilson (the U. Q) are convinced that INFINITE SPACE IS DOTTED WITH BALLS OF LIGHT, all of which are GALAXIES OF STARS and their orbiting planets.

THIS IS WHERE I COME IN TO SAY THEY ARE MISTAKEN.

It is true that at a distance both galaxies and galactic suns ARE BALLS OF LIGHT. But just as the REAL STARS in our planetary galaxy differentiate themselves from satellites and reflecting planets by their "TWINKLING, TWINKLING," if my colleague Cosmographers will be MORE ALERT, they will see that the light from the Galactic Suns IS MORE COMPACT as against the distorted-disjointed-BY –THE - SPACES- IN BETWEEN –THE-STARS, that constitute those BALLS OF LIGHT that are planetary galaxies.

Of course, but for the different star patterns we see with our own eyes, with every new MOON-CYCLE, it would have been very difficult to convince MANKIND that our planet orbits our sun over 364 days. Also, but for the DAY LIGHT that obliterates THE STARS, the very ROTATION OF OUR PLANET ON ITS AXIS would have assisted us in seeing ALL THE ZODIAC SIGNS every 24 hours.

WE have a 71 year ROTATING – ON- ITS- AXIS- PLANETARY- GALAXY to assist us in plotting all the GALACTIC SUNS as we use the telescopic camera to SNAP ALL THE BALLS OF LIGHT every day over a period of 71 years . Actually we need a minimum of TWO ROTATIONS of the planetary galaxy for us to separate the galactic suns from the galaxies- proper.

On the assumption that the Galactic Suns are STATIONARY whilst the PLANETARY GALAXIES are on the move inside our GALACTIC GALAXY, any discrepancy in the position of the BALLS OF LIGHT over a period of 142 years or even 284 years, will show us clearly the BALLS OF LIGHT that have remained in place as opposed to those balls of light that have EITHER MOVED AWAY FROM US or even COME CLOSER TO US!

The Galactic Solar System CONCEPT is also the only proper way to UNDERSTAND HUBBLE'S EFFECT, where approaching and RECEDING balls of light, confused past Cosmographers to construe an EXPANDING and a CONTRACTING UNIVERSE,

FALLACY. The same mistake which led them to postulate that most STUPID "BIG BANG" THEORY. I unhesitatingly call it STUPID because they need a PREVIOUSLY CREATED STAR SYSTEM to contract and HEAT UP to the point of EXPLOSION before CREATION CAN START-----Previously created-----to start-----(Very illogical)

With the use of THE LAW OF CORRESPONDENCE, we are only going to duplicate our planetary SOLAR SYSTEM and our planetary GALAXY with a GALACTIC solar system and a GALACTIC galaxy .

The LESSER ZODIAC we have in our planetary galaxy, will be duplicated by the GREATER ZODIAC in our GALACTIC GALAXY.

When our Cosmographers plot the positions of all the galactic suns over the next 71 years and compare the pictures-----date by date, year by year , with the PICTURES of the second 71 years, not only will they admit that indeed our galaxy rotates on its axis, but they will confirm that a day in the life of our planetary galaxy is equal to the LIFE SPAN of the average human being .

However, the Joke is on me given that l am no mathematician or geometrician. I took the liberty of dividing 26,000 years by our 364 days. There you are. I have given the detractors enough ammunition to turn me into a laughing stock.

If in our planetary solar system we have our planet orbiting its SUN / STAR and we want to do "AS ABOVE SO BELOW; AS BELOW SO ABOVE", then we must allow our planetary galaxy too, to orbit its Galactic sun in our Galactic Solar System.

If OPHIUCHUS and company constitute a part of the planetary galaxy (of stars and their orbiting planets), then the ELDER OPHIUCHUS up there in the SKY THAT WE CAN SEE IF WE STAND ON TOP OF THE PLANETARY GALAXY, must have its ELDER LIBRA, SCORPIO, TAURUS etc constituting what I choose to call THE GALACTIC GALAXY.

Infact, it is because of this CORRESPONDENCE POSSIBILITY that my writings have become awkward and cumbersome with the addition of the word 'PLANETARY' to what you already know to be simply 'SOLAR SYSTEM' and 'GALAXY'.

Humanity has become so used to the phrase 'GALAXY OF STARS' that, their need to know the TRUTH, enjoins me to point out to them that every STAR IS A SUN and every SUN / STAR has planets orbiting IT.

Therefore a GALAXY must necessarily be understood to be AN ISLAND OF STARS AND THEIR PLANETS in the ocean of infinite space, so that a galactic sun will become AN ISLAND OF LIGHT

A Galaxy must therefore be an ISLAND OF PLANETARY SOLAR SYSTEMS.

Because of the DOUBLE MOTION of our planet and the double motion of our galaxy and the possible double motion of the planetary galaxies of the other galactic solar systems in our Galactic Galaxy, maybe my colleague Cosmographers will need 284 years to be able to really know the Galactic Suns that constitute the Galactic Galaxy. But as soon as they succeed, even after 500 years, they should not hesitate to postulate, THE GALACTO GALACTIC GALAXY and the higher ones up to where l have visited these last TEN YEARS, in my SPIRIT: The Galacto- Galacto- Galacto- Galacto- Galacto- (i.e. to the fifth power) Galactic Galaxy.

I must confess that l have found a collaborator in the Master Max Heindel who has named my Galacto (5) Galactic Galaxy THE FIRST COSMIC PLANE on page 178 of his <u>Rosicrucian Cosmo Conception.</u>

He is my Henry Lincoln in this second exercise.

In today's meeting, our Galactic Solar System is going to have our own planetary galaxy imitating our planet in that our galaxy will be THE FOURTH from their galactic sun.

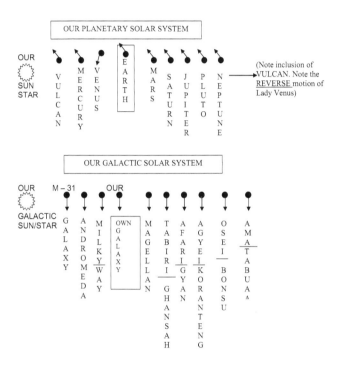

In our Galactic Solar System, our planet's 28-day journey through each ZODIAC SIGN is duplicated by our planetary galaxy's 2,000 year journey through each Greater Zodiac Sign.

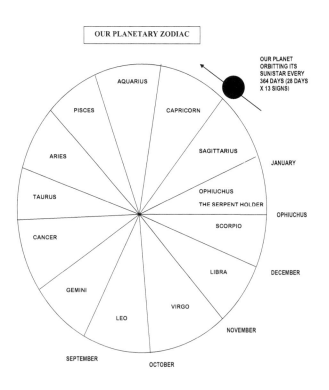

OUR PLANETARY ZODIAC

OUR PLANET
ORBITTING ITS
SUN/STAR EVERY
364 DAYS (28 DAYS
X 13 SIGNS)

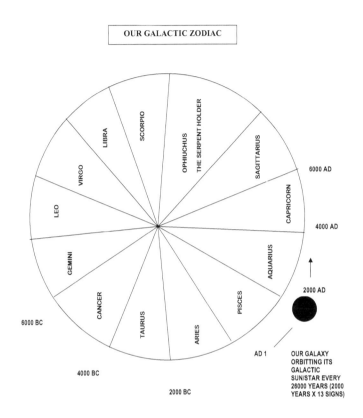

(Note that our galaxy moves majestically from PISCES to Aquarius as the planet does the opposite inside our galaxy. However, Jehovah and all his SONS and DAUGHTERS of Genesis Six, of the Venusian Capital city of RETZ , have the same Pisces to Aquarius scenario, since only VENUS has anti- clockwise direction inside our planetary solar system).

In our Galactic Solar System, our planet's 28-day journey through each ZODIAC SIGN is duplicated by our planetary galaxy's 2,000 year journey through each Greater Zodiac Sign.

* * *

Many Cosmographers erroneously believe that we are a part of the Milky Way Galaxy inspite of the fact that we have used The Hale Telescope to snap THE SIDE – VIEW PICTURE of this FLYING SAUCER- SHAPED Milky Way Galaxy . (In law of correspondence terms IT IS our ALPHA CENTAURI – our closest GALAXY NEIGHBOUR)

A picture of the Milky Way Galaxy can be found in Dr. Baldwin Baddoo's office. The very place where I first saw OPHIUCHUS written between Scorpio and Sagittarius on a MAP OF THE STARS.

I have right now, in front of me, the TOTAL MAP that I photocopied from Michael ZEILIK'S : ASTRONOMY – THE EVOLVING UNIVERSE (copyright 1988 – John Wiley

and Sons Inc) . I will make available all the five
photocopies as APPENDIX to this pamphlet.

*   *   *

So let us RECAPITULATE and say that the
NEW CONCEPT OF GALACTIC SUN explains
neatly why the Ancient Black Egyptians wrote
that there is a NEW AGE every 2000 years and
that the Greater Zodiac is 26,000 years long.
We do not need any PROMETHEAN show
whereby David ICKE tries to force Cinderella's
shoe on the foot of a PLEIDEAN CONCEPT
and the Master Max Heindel tries to force the
same shoe on a joke called THE PRECESSION
OF THE EQUINOXES. I call it a joke because
with the Precession of the Equinoxes, the AGE
OF AQUARIUS can be seen IN THE ROOF of
our own dear planetary galaxy, instead of in the
ROOF of our Galactic Galaxy

With the Galactic Solar System those who can
stand on top of the galaxy WITH ME , IN
SPIRIT , will see the Water Carrier dawning at
the ASCENDANT HORIZON as our infamous
AGE OF PISCES waves us goodbye at the

RECEDING HORIZON INSIDE THE ROOF OF OUR Galactic Galaxy.

The discerning reader must have realized by now that there is NOTHING LIKE A SEPARABLE planetary solar system throughout INFINITY.

INFINTE SPACE is " POPULATED" BY ONLY DISCERNIBLE BALLS OF LIGHT ----- DISCERNIBLE ISLANDS OF BALLS OF LIGHT

GALAXIES AND GALACTIC SUNS ARE THE SMALLEST POSSIBLE CELLS OF THE VOIDGOD ORGANISM.

Even if we choose to call all of them PLANETARY GALAXIES, Moses and Jehovah will have a hard time SHOWING US WHERE Jehovah created waters, plants, suns, moons, animals and humans, outside of galaxies AND ON SEPARATE DAYS, to boot.

In saying that Jehovah RESTED, Moses left us wondering whether the SABBATH DAY is still operative or inoperative.

The TRUTH is that INSTINCTGOD IS STILL IN THE BUSINESS OF MANIFESTING NEW GALACTO (5) GALACTIC GALAXIES, even as you read this line. Which means that another Galacto (5) Galactic Galaxy is DISSOLVING somewhere in the boondocks of INFINITY to ensure that THE DIVINE EQUILIBRIUM of The Galaxies –Cycle is never disturbed. Roy Eugene Davis " THE TEACHINGS OF THE MASTERS OF PERFECTION collaborates WITH ME ON EITHER PAGE 58 OR PAGE 156.

It is because there is no SEPARATE or SEPARABLE planetary solar system or no SEPARATE or SEPARABLE galactic solar system, that I INSIST that the smallest MOST STABLE UNIT/ CELL throughout INFINITY, must be the GALACTO (5) GALACTIC GALAXY. I hesitate in accepting THE GALAXY as the smallest most stable unit/ cell throughout INSTINCTVOIDGOD BECAUSE AT THIS MOMENT THAT YOU ARE READING THIS LINE, the INDEPENDENCE OF THE GALACTIC SOLAR SYSTEM is being questioned by The Galactic Galaxy IN WHICH it HAS BEEN TRAPPED. AND THE

GALACTIC Galaxy has also been trapped in its Galacto Galactic Galaxy.

If you are good in the MYSTIC ART OF CONTEMPLATION, then by now you are aware that the PLANET EARTH is not only trapped inside the planetary solar system, BUT IT IS ALSO LOCKED UP FIRMLY INSIDE THE PLANETARY GALAXY OF STARS AND PLANETS.

Of course, you may choose not to believe that OUR PLANETARY GALAXY is on the move around its sun. I will not blame you because you have never peeped through a telescope like The Hale Telescope, before. And you have not had the PRIVILEGE of seeing PICTURES of millions of millions of GALAXIES and GALACTIC SUNS that THE AETHERIUS SOCIETY (of Rev. Acquah, Mrs. Afro Gbedemah and Mrs. Rita Mark Coffie) shows to the public every now and then at the ACCRA BRITISH COUNCIL. I had my turn in 1995. So you see, I have seen pictures of the M-31,the Andromeda, the Milky Way, the Magellan, the Afari Gyan , the Ama Tabuaa, the Apostle Osei-Bonsu of Akuajoo-

Nkawkaw, GALAXIES and some GALACTIC SUNS.

If you are good in the Mystic Art of Contemplation, then by now NO ONE , NO FALSE HUMAN GOD, can frighten you with the IDEA that the planet can fall down into an abyss. There is no way even THE GALAXY can fall out of the Galactic Solar System let alone THE GALACTIC GALAXY. And the higher truth is that the Galaxies-Cycle is HERMETICALLY- SEALED in the same way that THE WATER –CYCLE is hermetically-sealed… in the same way that the God - Cycle is hermetically - sealed.

So you ARE ALL SAFE IN THE ARMS OF THE VOIDGOD OCEAN

Imagine the first Galacto-Galactic-Galaxy moving in an anti-clockwise direction inside the Galacto-Galacto-Galactic Solar System. Then imagine the Galactic Galaxy moving in a clockwise direction inside the Galacto Galactic Solar System. (I hope you are aware that the PLANET VENUS moves in an anti-clockwise direction inside our planetary Solar System.)

WHY, are you remembering John Lennon and how he LOVED just watching the Planetary, the Solar, the Galactic, the Galactic Galaxy, the Galacto-Galactic Galaxy WHEELS going round and round, because he loved to watch them ROLL, when he was no longer trapped on only the planet Earth's MERRY-GO-ROUND? (ON THE BALL by John Lennon. I am afraid his IMAGINE is threatening to come to pass within the next TEN YEARS.)

Then imagine again the Galaxy moving in an UPWARD direction inside the Galactic Solar System. Do not shake your head in DISBELIEF at the upward direction attributed to the galaxy. After all RAIN WATER does not FALL in Australia. IT RISES UPWARD towards the planet. (I gottcha.)

RAIN falls downwards in England and the Arctic area but comes towards us around the EQUATOR!

*   *   *

INSTINCTVOIDGOD knows that we have NO SAY as to whether we want to enter THE AQUARIAN AGE of our Galactic Galaxy or not ….. As to whether we want to enter THE OPHIUCHUS AGE of our Galacto Galactic Galaxy or not. Maybe our Galacto (5) Galactic Galaxy is now in its Age of LIBRA .Only Edgar Caycee can tell us which AGE we are really experiencing.

*   *   *

How did Edgar Caycee know in Warren SMITH'S <u>SECRET FORCES OF THE PYRAMIDS</u> that around this time, our planetary galaxy would move into an area of SPACE where the predominant GAS would not be TEAR GAS nor LAUGHING GAS, but FEARLESS THINKING GAS , which was going to STIMULATE those whose bodies were in harmony with NATURE to awaken from the HYPNOTIC SLUMBER that the Age of PISCES GAS had submerged all of us? (No guitarist can give of his best on an INSTRUMENT that is out of TUNE …… when you allow MEAT, ALCOHOL, CIGARETTES, EXCESS SEX, ANGER, JEALOUSY, THEOLOGY AND RACISM to disorient you……).

Our galaxy has moved into the RAINY SEASON of the Galactic Solar System (do you remember those Rainy Seasons inside the planetary solar system …. and my stones?) and there is nothing Jehovah, Jesus, Krishna, the Buddha or any of our Spiritual Masters OF PAST AGES, can do about the MENTAL and SPIRITUAL FREEDOM predestined for all of us.

Just as NO FORCE can withstand the RESOLVE of a DETERMINED SOUL, NO GOD, Euroamerican, Arab, Indian, Japanese or WHATEVER, can stop an OPHIUCHUS; Galactic Solar System; Galaxies cycle; God cycle; SUBCONSCIOUS – MIND – AS – THE – GOD – WITHIN – THAT – ALWAYS – CREATES – US – IN – THE – IMAGE – WE – IMPRINT – ON – IT – WITH – OUR – BELIEFS; (IT WILL ALWAYS CREATE YOU IN ITS OWN IMAGE); Intentional Self – Denials, CONCEPTS, whose TIME HAS COME.

*   *   *

Since the Master Max Heindel has been KIND enough to show us the Galacto (5) Galactic

Galaxy as ALL THAT THERE IS throughout
INFINITY, let me be KINDER still and tell
him that he ERRS, abysmally.

His Galacto(5) Galactic Galaxy is but ONE of
some 700million Galacto(5) Galactic Galaxies
that I have visited IN MY SPIRIT, these past ten
years. And they are all A PART of the eternally
SELF – RENEWING, self – transforming,
Galaxies – Cycle that is hermetically – sealed
and IMMUTABLE, in the GOD – CYCLE .
There is NO BEGINNING TO God so stop
taking Moses serious. There is no LAST
JUDGEMENT either. Lazarus and the Rich
man did not wait for this JOKE.

The GODUNIVERSE ENSHROUDS/
INCORPORATES THE 700 MILLION
GALACTO(5) GALACTIC GALAXIES IN
ETERNAL UNFOLDMENT/EVOLUTION.
Eric Van Lustbader is very good at meditating
beyond THE MATERIAL HALF of the God –
Cycle. He is capable of ENTERING THE VOID
HALF where the ACTION really IS. All the
Masters who have attained this TECHNIQUE
and DEGREE yawn at the TRANSIENT nature
of even the Galacto (5) Galactic Galaxies.

THE VOID disgorges everything.

THE VOID swallows up everything.

No condition in Materiality is PERMANENT.

That is why NO MASTER HANKERS AFTER so – called beautiful faces in NATURE. They know the destination of all girls IS THAT OLD WOMAN who is toothless, to boot! No Master is DELUDED. No Master harbours DESIRES. No Master is HOSTILE against MANIFESTATIONS OF INSTINCT.

Infact, the OMNIPRESENT, OMNIPOTENT, OMNISCIENT INSTINCTVOIDGOD ORGANISM, whose eternally self – transforming BODY is what is going on in the INFINITE INSTINCTVOIDGOD OVERSOUL (AURA) as the Galaxies – Cycle, IS ALL THAT GOD IS ABOUT throughout INFINITY and ETERNITY. The more so since ALL VISIBLE MATTER is not only TIME – SENSITIVE but also BIODEGRADABLE – SENSITIVE, back into their INVISIBLE atomic and molecular states which never CEASE COMING BACK into materiality, only to be BROKEN DOWN AGAIN, to build up again, AD INFINITUM. (You are a MICRO GOD, the trouble being your IGNORANCE of your SUBCONSCIOUS – MIND – HYPNOSIS POWERS)

Go peep into THE MICROSCOPE and you will see that there is NO BREAK between the fertilized EGG, the dying man and the RESURRECTED GHOST that also grows YOUNG in the Spiritual Realms (at ASAMANDO), to be CONCEIVED AGAIN , before being BORN AGAIN as a CHILD.

HAVE YOU EVER CONTEMPLATED IN WONDER, as WOOD smoke, METAL smoke, OIL smoke, BURNT ANIMAL Smoke, BURNT HUMAN smoke, ALL RISE INTO THE SKY TO FALL BACK AS RAIN? Have you ever MEDITATED UPON THIS WATER under the MICROSCOPE, to see how all the AMOEBA, PROTOZOA, GERMS OR VIRUSES end up evolving back into whatever THEY WERE BEFORE THEY WERE BURNT UP?

IN MY WORLD I DO NOT NEED WHITE GODS, BLACK GODS, INDIAN GODS OR ANY HUMAN GOD, BEFORE MY ONE OMNIPRESENT, OMNISCIENT, OMNI-POTENT, INSTINCTGOD CONTINUES ETERNALLY AND INFINITELY, WITH MANIFESTATIONS OF ALL VARIETIES. (YOU CAN BURN UP ALL THE STARS AND PLANETS THAT CONSTITUTE OUR GALAXY ……….. AND STILL GET THE SAME STARS AND PLANETS TO RE – EMERGE ……….. BECAUSE THE GENETIC BLUEPRINT IS INDESTRUCTIBLE.)(EVERY THING SHALL PASS BUT THE GENETIC WORD OF THE GOD – CYCLE WILL ETERNALLY – INFINITELY RE – MANIFEST)

The human life – cycle is as hermetically – sealed as the Water – Cycle and the Galaxies – Cycle. And we can lump it all into the God – Cycle. EVERYTHING IS GOD IN MANIFESTATION .Everything : The animals, the trees, the humans, everything. There is NOTHING like a CREATION OF GOD. The problem is that you have never witnessed a HYPNOTIST IN ACTION. With the SUBCONSCIOUS – MIND, EVERYTHING IS POSSIBLE. EVERYTHING.

Go peep into the MICROSCOPE and you will see Galaxies and Galacto (5) Galactic Galaxies at the GENETIC – BLUEPRINT – INVISIBLE – TO

–THE – EYE FORMATIVE STAGES, IN THE INSTINCTVOIDGOD OCEAN.

IT IS IN IT(IN THIS INSTINCT OCEAN) THAT GALAXIES MOVE, LIVE AND HAVE THEIR

BEINGS WITH ALL OF US CRAWLING ON THEIR BACKS AS MOTHERLESS AND FATHERLESS MELCHIZEDEKS AND ROMULUS AND REMUS ETC ETC. NOT IN ANY HIM CALLED JEHOVAH, JESUS, KRISHNA or any such product like yourself.

If you realize your SUBCONSCIOUS – MIND SPIRITUAL POWERS, GREATER THINGS than WHAT Jesus, Jehovah did, YE SHALL DO! !

To equate any HUMAN BEING or even any PAST or PRESENT GOD – REALIZED MASTER, to the Spiritual Omnipotent, Omnipresent, Omniscient, INSTINCTGOD, is to display the greatest SPIRITUAL IGNORANCE. If you do that you will be forced to put human GODS INTO ANTS and TREES and ANIMALS and FERTILIZED EGGS before INSTINCTGOD CAN SEE TO THEIR UNFOLDMENT. THE BRUTAL TRUTH IS THAT GOD IS EVERYTHING BOTH VISIBLE AND INVISIBLE

There is more MUSIC in the invisible SILENCE and there are more COLOURFUL IMAGES in the invisible VOIDNESS, that even a human contraption like the television can make PLAIN TO US.

You can develop your CLAIRAUDIENT and CLAIRVOYANT POTENTIALS WITHIN YOUR SUBCONSCIOUS INSTINCT MIND and end up laughing at those YOU HAVE BEEN WORSHIPPING. When you become a MASTER in the ART OF INTENTIONAL SELF – DENIALS and you attain SUPERCONSCIOUSNESS

"When we attain superconsciousness before physical death, death does not stop our AWARENESS. We re – incarnate consciously and come to do OPHIUCHUS and Galactic Solar System and God – Cycle unveiling, CONSCIOUSLY. (It's only a way of speaking. I am far from superconsciousness. But God knows I have removed myself from IMPULSIVE – INSTINCTIVE BEHAVIOUR into CONSCIOUS, CONTROLLED, DISCIPLINED REACTIONS. I always LOOK BEFORE I LEAP. I AM TOO INTELLIGENT NOT TO THINK BEFORE ACTING. Those of you who are SLAVES TO IMPULSIVE REACTIONS are indeed a PITIABLE LOT. Your lives are so UGLY, from the human point of view. So, please start practising Intentional Self – Denials. It is the wisest way to LIVE.) Only man as superconscious man KNOWS that even material achievements are things that keep us EARTH – BOUND " (P 162)

- <u>Deeper Man</u> by : J.G Bennett with interpolation.-

THE GOD – PHENOMENON HAS NO BEGINNING NOR ENDING.

There is nothing like a BIG – BANG BEGINNING. There is no such thing as an END TO SPACE OR AN END TO TIME. Forget it. It is AN IMPOSSIBILITY in the God – Scheme – Of – Things . SCARRY AS IT IS, it is the only possibility there is. That makes GOD UNKNOWABLE, AWESOME,AWE – INSPIRING and INEFFABLE. There is no way a FINITE MIND can comprehend AN INFINITE LIVING MIND.

As indicated earlier, Hubble's Effect speaks as if GOD CAN EXPAND today and CONTRACT tomorrow and EXPAND …….. Expand to where? And what lies beyond THAT BOUNDARY YOU HAVE DRAWN TO LIMIT GOD, THE ILLIMITABLE?

Look here, THERE HAS NEVER BEEN and THERE WILL NEVER BE A TIME WHEN GOD IS NOT GOD! God has never RESTED for even a micro second. God has never slept for even a micro second. As for those who speak as if God can die for THREE LONG DAYS, the least said about that scenario, the better. (ONYAME ⊃NT ⊃ NKO, NA W' ADA)

There has never been and there will never be A MOMENT IN TIME, or A PLACE IN SPACE or A CONDITION IN CHANGE, where the INSTINCTVOIDGOD- VISIBLEGALAXIESGOD balance, is not IMMANENT. There is no way INSTINCTGOD can be LESS THAN IT IS or MORE THAN IT IS .THE ALL IS immutable. It IS composed OF THE SAME number of galacto (5) galaxy cells, all the time.

As one Galacto (5) Galactic Galaxy dissolves this side of infinite space, another Galacto (5) Galactic Galaxy emerges FROM THE VOID on the other side of Infinite space TO MAINTAIN THE DIVINE EQUILIBRIUM ETERNALLY- INFINITELY.

There has never been and there will never be a TIME when THE ALL IS ONLY THE VOID HALF! Forget about the BIG BANG which needs a PRE- CREATED- STAR - SYSTEM anyway, before it can be operative. Pre- created by WHAT or by WHOM?

If you MEDITATE OVER THE WATER –CYCLE you will come to understand not only the Galaxies-Cycle, the God –cycle and the LIFE- CYCLE, but you will attain spiritual sobriety by humbly accepting that you can never HAVE A HUMAN BEING, AS GOD.

When you attain that humility, you will hesitate to say that GOD IS A WHITE MAN or that he slept with somebody's betrothed wife, to get A BEGOTTEN SON.

You see, these people do not SHARE THE MYSTICAL REVERENCE that those of us who have CONTEMPLATED THE MYSTERIOUS VOID have for THE ALL. They are THEOLOGICAL but never RELIGIOUS. That THE ALL is a JEALOUS GOD? Jealous of WHOM? "As Above So Below ; As Below So Above" teaches me that just as NO DROP OF WATER(W) is lost to the water –cycle, NO drop of Matter (m) is lost to the Galaxies-Cycle. By extension NO SOUL SPARK(S) OF THE ALL is lost to the God-Cycle.

As the Earth's Ocean loses water through evaporation, THE Earth's Sky gains that specific volume of water. When rain falls, rises or whatever, IT TEACHES ME THAT NOT A DROP OF WATER IS EVER LOST TO THE WATER-CYLE.

Always CONTEMPLATE MY FAVOURITE EXAMPLE. It is what has made it possible for me to smile when I hear" I believe in God the Father Almighty, Maker of Heaven and Earth, and in HIS ONLY BEGOTTEN SON Jesus Christ blah, blah, blah. "

Like "Thirty days hath September..." the above belief is only fit for the primary school of OUR SPIRITUAL EDUCATION. And because there are some among us who CAN NEVER READ, and because there are some among us who are afraid of FAT BOOKS, and because there are some among us who are AFRAID TO THINK (not to talk of THINKING FEARLESSLY)...... you deserve to be congratulated if you have read THIS FAR.

FORTUNATELY FOR Jehovah, Jesus, Allah, Krishna and all the PAST MASTERS WHO HAVE BEEN DEIFIED by the IGNORANT MAJORITY, l see them as PAST AVATARAS

WHO HAD HUMAN ANIMALS TO
EDUCATE.

WHAT WOULD HAVE HAPPENED TO
THE GALACTIC SOLAR SYSTEM IDEA IF
THERE WERE NO TELESCOPES TO LEND
ME CREDENCE?

WHAT WOULD HAVE HAPPENED TO
THE GENES- GENETIC- INSTINCT- writing
–moving- finger- of- God (Omar Khayyam)
IF THERE WERE NO MICROSCOPES TO
LEND ME CREDENCE?

And as for those who think COLONIALISM
and NEO- COLONIALISM are our enemies,
compare the roads, the houses, the electricity,
the pipe borne – water, the hospitals, the school,
to the natural resources they have taken away
as RECOMPENSE, and come back to tell me
that we have NOT GAINED.

At least, colonialism has been bitten by
DIALECTICAL MATERIALISM to produce
Amorifer

I remember EGYPT as if it were only yesterday. We had degenerated as ALL MATERIAL PHENOMENA must. Our heritage was in danger of being irretrievably lost. Like America is doing now with VISA LOTTERY and BRAIN DRAIN FROM ELSEWHERE, to stem her degeneration, EGYPT LOST OUT TO THE LAW OF RHYTHM. Hermes took an lsraeli KID (MOSES) WHO WAS HUNGRY FOR KNOWLEDGE.

How many American Kids are hungry for knowledge when they are compared to African kids who will sell the family COCOA FARM just to get to America? Nothing MATERIAL escapes NATURAL LAW. The law of Karma ENSURES THAT EVERY OPHIUCHUS-DENIED- EXISTENCE, IS UNVEILED , not by the WHITE BLOCKS that are already in the super-structure, but by the BLACK BLOCK that was rejected and condemned as USELESS.

WHOSOEVER KNOWS BIOLOGY KNOWS THAT THE TADPOLE(KONKONTIBANE) IS ACTUALLY PREDESTINED TO BE THE FROG. AND THAT THE CATERPILLAR, (THE CATERPILLAR CALLED THE BLACK

RACE) IS ACTUALLY PREDESTINED TO BE THE SOARING BUTTERFLY.

GOD WILL UNFOLD AS IT IS PREDESTINED TO . THOSE WHO KNOW THE GENETIC CODE OF GOD KNOW THAT THE AGE OF AQUARIUS IS THE **AGE OF PUBERTY FOR THE GODSEED**.

So I embrace, **IN ALL LOVE**, Allah, Jehovah, Jesus, Krishna as Worthy Divine Petty Tyrant Opponents (according to Carlos Castaneda's books) who were harassing us under the direct instructions of their own INSTINCTS planted in their GENES by the INSTINCT GOD ITSELF(THE ONLY TYRANT-according to Don Juan Matus).

After all I was PREDESTINED to be AMORIFER. The more **INSTINCTVOIDGOD CHANGES** (even into SMOKE) the more INSTINCTGOD remains the same, by bouncing BACK INSTINCTIVELY!

INSTINCTGODORGANISM Is always the same at all POINTS IN TIME, at all SPOTS IN SPACE , under ALL CONDITIONS IN CHANGE.

Nature is only spared needless MISUNDERSTANDING , confusion, anxiety, pain and suffering if things are worked upon through the introduction of INTENTIONAL SELF-DENIALS by the OPHIUCHUS-UNVEILING- AVATARA called Amorifer.

GOD HAS A BLUEPRINT. EVEN IF YOU GET TO KNOW IT, you will have to transform yourself through Intentional Self – Denials to remove yourself from INSTINCTIVE BEHAVIOUR to be able to ENJOY ITS EVOLUTION.

GOD WILL UNFOLD INSTINCTIVELY ETERNALLY IF WE DO NOT RESIST INSTINCTIVE BEHAVIOUR.
"Perhaps our blindness to the importance of the DENYING (NEGATIVE) FORCE is most forcibly seen in the difficulty we have equating the cosmic roles of GOD THE SON and SATAN. They are essentially the same but because Satan (has been painted as) the adversary, the very personification of the denying force, we find it terribly hard not to think him as negative.

Yet, without TEMPTATION TO DO GOOD OR EVIL (as the priest in the Good Samaritan story was TEMPTED TO DO GOOD, but failed) and without the force of RESISTANCE TO ALL INSTINCTIVE DIVINE IMPULSES, the transformation of INDIVIDUALS would not be possible- and the SELF- IMPROVEMENT PURPOSE OF MANIFESTATION IN NATURE, could not be fulfilled. It is through our own DENIAL (Self –Denial, Self – sacrifice) that we are able to TRANSFORM INTO BETTER PEOPLE." (P 143)

Deeper Man: J.G.Bennett

Greetings from my Spiritual Guide Hermes Trismegistus, who was also in Egypt when we gave HAGAR…..IS HMAEL…to Abraham. Our grandchildren are now SAYING OUR LAND IS NOT OUR LAND .

They are chasing the Sisters and Brothers of Hagar from DARFUR too, after stealing Egypt, Libya, Tunisia, Algeria, Morocco , Mauritania, The Sudan, with their ISLAMIC JIHAD after the death of Mohammed.

Paul Brunton, you said it in A SEARCH IN
SECRET EGYPT.

The SPHINX smiled at the planting of the
GREEN FLAG of ISLAM – (the flag of
ARABIZATION) when CHRISTIANIZED
EGYPT (EUROPEANIZED EGYPT, really)
of Pope Arius of Alexandria, (the one who said
NO to the changing of Jesus into a GOD at the
Council of Nicea – Constantinopole – present
day Istanbul of Turkey in 325 A.D.) lost out.

The ungrateful "Young man, GO East to Egypt
for learning and Wisdom" Greeks, thanked
Egypt by biting the hand that fed them! (Today
they will GO SOUTH TO EGYPT).

When someone saw that the Greek CAMBYSES
INVASION was leading to the loss of the Coptic
and Hieroglyphic SCRIPTS, he composed THE
ROSETTA STONE. -The vertical arrangement
of the corresponding alphabets of the Greek, the
Coptic and the Hieroglyphics

Napoleon also invaded Egypt and could not stand
the NEGROID FLAT NOSE and the NEGROID
THICK LIPS OF THE SPHINX . . . Boys, fire!

(Quel dommage). Ils ont vraiment change notre chanson.(Look what they have done to our NEGROID SPHINX now) (ARABIC NOSE).

The Saudi Arabian woman who was using The Rosetta Stone as a GRINDING STONE at the Port City of Rosetta, near Alexandria – Egypt.

That Captain in Napoleon's army prompted by the GODINSTINCT WITHIN to purchase THE ROSETTA STONE. . . which is now at The Museum in London.

Champolion and the TRANSCRIBING OF LUCIFER'S Alexandrian and Memphis LIBRARY BOOKS into the EUROPEAN LANGUAGES after using the Rosetta as Master Key. . . why they get to know about Galaxies in 1920.

The sudden EXPLOSION of Science and technology in Euroamerica in the Nineteenth century. If Agnew knew then Nixon knew. The French ought to be ashamed of themselves. They have known THE ALPHA and ZETA all this while. They know they owe their science and technology to LUCIFER'S BOOKS.

Why do the Greek also say Alpha and Omega when they know that their Alphabet ends with ZETA? (poor Revelations 21:6 and 22:13)

The beginning and the end can never be The Alpha and Omega.The Alpha and Zeta is THE CORRECT VERSION.

HYPNOTIZED TO ACCEPT THE FALSE AS THE TRUTH...even in their Christian Bible!

*   *   *

If you understand Ecclesiastes 7:13, and you try to live the TRUTH THEREIN, you will never expect medical students to BEHAVE LIKE FULLY FLEDGED DOCTORS. THE EVOLUTION OF THE GOD SEED follows the processes of the Evolution of the HUMAN SEED. Ecclesiastes 3:1-8 is GOD IN UNFOLDMENT. WHEN IT IS GOD'S TIME TO FALSIFY... TO REINSTATE FALSIFIED TRUTHS! GO READ DESIDERATA. . . AND BE AT PEACE WITH GOD WHATEVER YOUR CONCEPTION OF IT . . . THE SPIRITUAL NON-HUMAN GOD. THE GODUNIVERSE IS UNFOLDING AS IT SHOULD ...... SO BE AT PEACE WITH GOD.

IF THE MIGHTY OCEAN OF GOD IS UNCREATED, THEN THE DROPS OF GOD ESSENCE, GOD WATER, GOD MATTER, GOD MENTAL SUBSTANCE THAT MAKE THE MIGHTY GOD OCEAN ARE UNCREATED…SO BE AT PEACE WITH THE MANIFESTED AND UNMANIFESTED ASPECTS OF THE HERMETICALLY-SEALED VOIDGODWHOLE.

Nothing is a CREATION of God.

Everything is a MANIFESTATION of God.

POSTLUDE TO BOOK TWO

THE LAW OF LOVE

"Your ability to transform the (mental) world will depend on your ability to TRANSFORM YOURSELF .

Your power, success, and degree of attainment of this secret will depend on this ONE CONDITION:

THAT YOU CONTINUE TO MAINTAIN AN OPEN MIND, A BROAD AND TOLERANT ASPECT OF LIFE AND THOSE WHO LIVE, AND PERMIT NO SHACKLES OR CHAINS OF (THEOLOGICAL) CREEDS AND DOGMAS, FORMS AND NARROW CONVENTIONAL THOUGHTS TO TIE YOU TO EARTHLY THOUGHTS AND BIGOTED LIVING.

YOUR MIND AND HEART MUST BE AS BROAD, AS TOLERANT, AS KIND, AS GENEROUS, AS CONSIDERATE, AS THE COSMIC.

YOUR WILLINGNESS TO FORGIVE, TO OVERLOOK WEAKNESSES, TO CONDONE ERRORS, TO HOLD OUT A HAND TO THOSE WHO SEEM TO FALL, MUST EQUAL THE SPIRIT WITHIN THE HEARTS AND SOULS OF THE GREAT MASTERS TO WHOM YOU WILL NOW APPEAL AND WITH WHOM YOU WILL NOW ATTUNE YOURSELF AS NEVER BEFORE.

LOVE IS THE ONLY ESSENCE OF EXISTENCE.

LOVE IS THE MOST DYNAMIC FORCE IN THE UNIVERSE.

LOVE IS THE ONLY RULE AND GUIDE IN JUDGING, GIVING, VIEWING, RE-VIEWING, SENSING, UNDERSTANDING AND COM-PREHENDING EVERYONE AND EVERYTHING THAT EXISTS.

With this ATTITUDE you will remain powerful-Otherwise you will find your POWER WEAKENING continually, And the Law of RESPONSE, will fail to work for you"(It is not easy ------ but try to live IT-)

Printed in Great Britain
by Amazon